# Meet the
# WASHINGTON
# REDSKINS

## BY
## ZACK BURGESS

NORWOODHOUSE🏠PRESS

CHICAGO, ILLINOIS

# NORWOODHOUSE🏠PRESS

P.O. Box 316598 • Chicago, Illinois 60631
For more information about Norwood House Press please visit our website at
www.norwoodhousepress.com or call 866-565-2900.

Photo Credits:
All photos courtesy of Associated Press, except for the following: Topps, Inc. (6, 10 bottom, 11 top & middle),
Black Book Archives (7, 15, 18, 22), Bowman Gum Co. (10 top), Sports Illustrated for Kids (11 bottom),
Panini America (23).

Cover Photo: James D. Smith/Associated Press

The football memorabilia photographed for this book is part of the authors' collection. The collectibles used
for artistic background purposes in this series were manufactured by many different card companies—
including Bowman, Donruss, Fleer, Leaf, O-Pee-Chee, Pacific, Panini America, Philadelphia Chewing Gum,
Pinnacle, Pro Line, Pro Set, Score, Topps, and Upper Deck—as well as several food brands, including
Crane's, Hostess, Kellogg's, McDonald's and Post.

Designer: Ron Jaffe
Series Editors: Mike Kennedy and Mark Stewart
Project Management: Black Book Partners, LLC.
Editorial Production: Lisa Walsh

LIBRARY OF CONGRESS CATALOGING-IN-PUBLICATION DATA
  Names: Burgess, Zack.
  Title: Meet the Washington Redskins / by Zack Burgess.
  Description: Chicago Illinois : Norwood House Press, [2016] | Series: Big
    picture sports | Includes bibliographical references and index.
  Identifiers: LCCN 2015023114| ISBN 9781599537467 (library edition : alk.
    paper) | ISBN 9781603578493 (ebook)
  Subjects: LCSH: Washington Redskins (Football team)--History--Juvenile
    literature. | Washington Redskins (Football team)--Miscellanea.
  Classification: LCC GV956.W3 B87 2016 | DDC 796.332/6409753--dc23
  LC record available at http://lccn.loc.gov/2015023114

288N—072016
Manufactured in the United States of America in North Mankato, Minnesota

# CONTENTS

Words in **bold type** are defined on page 24.

The Redskins celebrate a great play.

4

# Call Me a Redskin

The Washington Redskins were named more than 80 years ago. Some believe their name honors Native American warriors. Others feel it is an insult to these proud people. The players continue to do what they have always done. They play with great heart.

# TIME MACHINE

In 1937, the Redskins played their first season in Washington, D.C. That year, they were crowned champions of the National Football League (NFL). From 1982 to 1991, the Redskins won the Super Bowl three times. Coach Joe Gibbs led those great teams. **John Riggins** was among his best players.

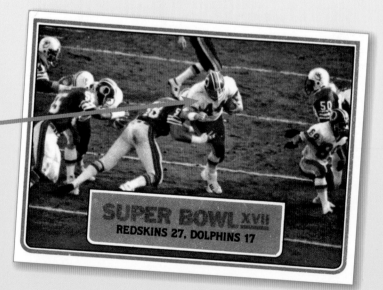

SUPER BOWL XVII
REDSKINS 27, DOLPHINS 17

Joe Gibbs was one of the smartest coaches ever.

There are no bad seats at the Redskins' stadium.

# Best Seat in the House

The Redskins' stadium used to be one of the largest in the NFL. Over the years, the team got rid of seats that were too far away from the field. Even so, Washington fans make the stadium one of the loudest in football.

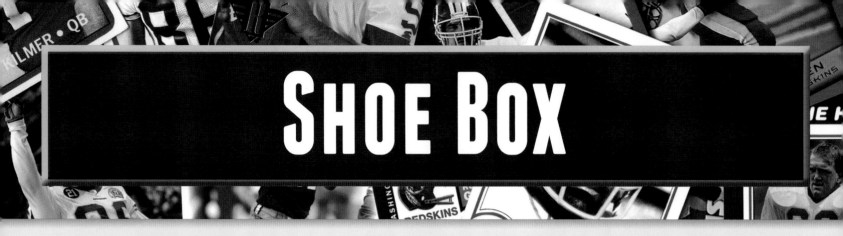

# SHOE BOX

The trading cards on these pages show some of the best Redskins ever.

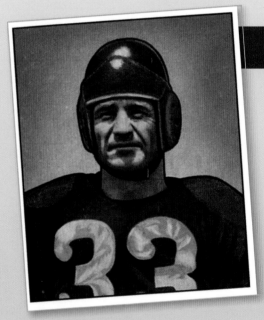

## SAMMY BAUGH

### QUARTERBACK & PUNTER · 1937-1952

"Slingin'" Sammy got his nickname because of how he threw the ball. His average of 45.1 yards per punt was an NFL record for more than 70 years.

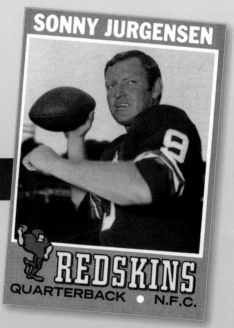

## SONNY JURGENSEN

### QUARTERBACK · 1964-1974

Sonny had a powerful arm. He loved to throw long "bombs" to speedy receivers.

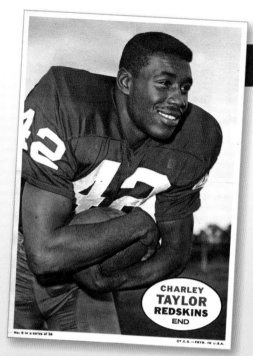

## CHARLEY TAYLOR

### RECEIVER · 1964 –1977

Charley was a great runner after the catch. He was picked for the **Pro Bowl** eight times during his career.

## ART MONK

### RECEIVER · 1980-1993

Art caught 888 passes for the Redskins. He was voted into the **Hall of Fame** in 2008.

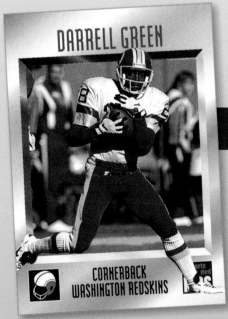

## DARRELL GREEN

### CORNERBACK · 1983-2002

Darrell was the fastest player in the NFL. He had at least one **interception** 19 seasons in a row.

# THE BIG PICTURE

Look at the two photos on page 13. Both appear to be the same. But they are not. There are three differences. Can you spot them?

*Answers on page 23.*

13

# TRUE OR FALSE?

Joe Theismann was a star quarterback. Two of these facts about him are **TRUE**. One is **FALSE**. Do you know which is which?

 1. Joe wore a one-bar facemask on his helmet.

 2. Joe threw more touchdown passes with his left hand than with his right.

 3. Joe was the NFL's Most Valuable Player (MVP) in 1983.

*Answer on page 23.*

Joe Theismann led the Redskins to a Super Bowl win.

Fans high-five the Redskins as they take the field.

# Go Redskins, Go!

On game day, the parking lot at the Redskins' stadium is filled with cars from all over the Southeast. The fans are loud and proud. They love to sing "Hail to the Redskins." It has been the team's fight song since 1938.

17

# ON THE MAP

Here is a look at where five Redskins were born, along with a fun fact about each.

 **1** · **CHARLES MANN · SACRAMENTO, CALIFORNIA**
Charles had more than 80 **quarterback sacks** for the Redskins.

 **2** · **MARK MOSELEY · LANEVILLE, TEXAS**
Mark was the first kicker to be named NFL MVP.

 **3** · **CLINTON PORTIS · LAUREL, MISSISSIPPI**
Clinton was a shifty runner and popular teammate.

 **4** · **STEPHEN DAVIS · SPARTANBURG, SOUTH CAROLINA**
Stephen led the NFL with 17 touchdowns in 1999.

 **5** · **ROBERT GRIFFIN III · OKINAWA PREFECTURE, JAPAN**
"RGIII" was an exciting player with a great nickname.

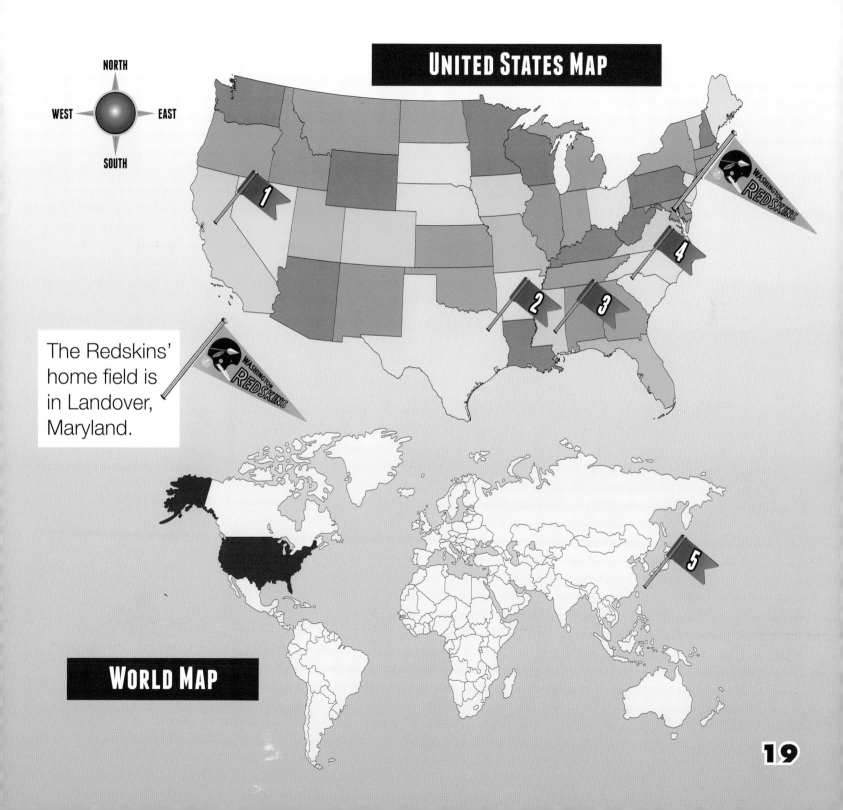

# UNITED STATES MAP

NORTH
WEST — EAST
SOUTH

The Redskins' home field is in Landover, Maryland.

# WORLD MAP

# Home and Away

Jordan Reed wears the Redskins' home uniform.

Football teams wear different uniforms for home and away games. The main colors of the Redskins are burgundy and gold. Burgundy is a dark shade of red.

Ryan Kerrigan wears the Redskins' away uniform.

The Redskins' helmet is burgundy with gold and white stripes. On each side, there is a picture of a Native American. The team has used a version of this logo since 1972.

The Redskins have won five NFL titles. Two came in the years before the Super Bowl, in 1937 and 1942. The Redskins later won the Super Bowl three times. They had a different quarterback each year: Joe Theismann, Doug Williams, and **Mark Rypien**.

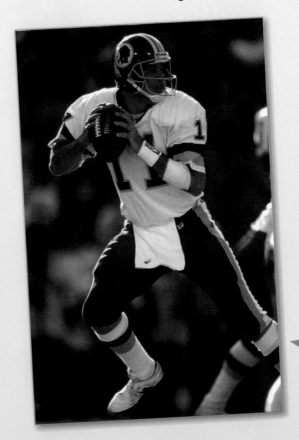

# RECORD BOOK

These Redskins set team records.

ROOKIE · ALFRED MORRIS · REDSKINS
SCORE 12

| TOUCHDOWN PASSES | RECORD |
|---|---|
| Season: Sonny Jurgensen (1967) | 31 |
| Career: Sammy Baugh | 187 |

| RUSHING YARDS | RECORD |
|---|---|
| Season: **Alfred Morris** (2012) | 1,613 |
| Career: John Riggins | 7,472 |

| INTERCEPTIONS | RECORD |
|---|---|
| Season: Dan Sandifer (1948) | 13 |
| Career: Darrell Green | 54 |

**ANSWERS FOR THE BIG PICTURE**
#46 changed to #12, the goal posts disappeared, and #68's pants stripe changed colors.

**ANSWER FOR TRUE AND FALSE**
#2 is false. Joe never threw a touchdown pass with his left hand.

# FOOTBALL WORDS

# INDEX

### Hall of Fame
The museum in Canton, Ohio, where football's greatest players are honored.

### Interception
A pass caught by a defensive player.

### Pro Bowl
The NFL's annual all-star game.

### Quarterback Sacks
Tackles of the quarterback that lose yardage.

Photos are on **BOLD** numbered pages.

## ABOUT THE AUTHOR

**Zack Burgess** has been writing about sports for more than 20 years. He has lived all over the country and interviewed lots of All-Pro football players, including Brett Favre, Eddie George, Jerome Bettis, Shannon Sharpe, and Rich Gannon. Zack was the first African American beat writer to cover Major League Baseball when he worked for the *Kansas City Star*.

## ABOUT THE REDSKINS

Learn more at these websites:
www.redskins.com  •  www.profootballhof.com
www.teamspiritextras.com/Overtime/html/redskins.html